Words in the Wilderness

Letters to My Bride

Lorene Masters Ness

Master Moments Books

For more information: lorenemasters@gmail.com

First paperback edition September 2022

ISBN 978-1-7373861-1-7

Dedication

The following words are for all in the body of Christ who are preparing for His return. I pray men and women alike will be blessed for He has called us all His Bride.

Originally, these words were written for a women's retreat, but they can be used as devotionals to read daily or several at a time.

A special thank you to Tani Parker for allowing me to share what the Lord has given me. Your reward will be great in Heaven!

Introduction

If you are going through a wilderness time, know that you are not alone! Many who have gone before us now attest that the Lord was there amid the suffering and loneliness. Though the enemy of our soul torments us, the Lord always has a set time for the trial of testing to end. Seek Him in your pain and uncertainty when it feels like friends are nowhere to be found. No testing time is wasted. Someday, all God-ordained trials will turn to gold in our eternal home.

If you have not yet met the Savior of your soul, let me introduce Him to you. The Bible says that all have sinned and fallen short of the glory of God. We have a sin problem, and Jesus solved that for us by dying on the cross for our sins, raising to life, and thus conquering sin for all mankind. We only have to come to Him, confess our sins, and accept the new life that He offers us. It is a new life that does not end when we die but continues for all eternity. The alternative is a life separated from Him and all life in Hell.

I pray the words in this book will minister to you as you continue through the wilderness of earth. And that you will see Jesus holding your hand, helping you stand firm, leading you through the sometimes-thick darkness of the wilderness. When it is hard to see the light, continue in the path He is making for you. The arduous journey will end, and the light will shine again. Be encouraged, His love has made a way for us to know Him today and for all eternity.

Lorene

"Hallelujah! For the Lord our God, the Almighty reigns! Let us rejoice and exalt Him and give Him glory because the wedding celebration of the Lamb has come. And His bride has made herself ready. Fine linen, shining bright and clear, has been given to her to wear, and the fine linen is the righteous deeds of His holy believers. Then the angel said to me, "Write these words: Wonderfully blessed are those who are invited to feast at the wedding celebration of the Lamb!" And then he said to me, "These are the true words of God." Revelations 19:7-91

"Then in a vision, I saw a new heaven and a new earth. The first heaven and earth had passed away, and the sea no longer existed. I saw the Holy City, the New Jerusalem, descending out of the heavenly realm from the presence of God, like a pleasing bride that had been prepared for her husband, adorned for her wedding." Revelation 21:1-3

"Come," says the Holy Spirit and the Bride in a divine duet. Let everyone who hears this duet join them in saying, "Come." Let everyone gripped with spiritual thirst say, "Come." And let everyone who craves the gift of living water come and drink it freely. "Come." Revelation 22:17

I love you

My precious child, I see what you cannot see. I know the motivation behind your actions that bring trouble to your soul. I long to bring healing to your memories. Some memories might be hidden from you, but I see them all and long to heal you.

When you do things that are hard to understand, I understand completely.

I am calling you to come to Me. Together we can look at the pain of the past. Tell Me where it hurts, where you feel angry or misunderstood. We will move together into the future. It is full of peace and joy. Never will I leave you, just as I never left you in the past. At times it may have felt like I abandoned you for a moment. Your pain may have caused My face to appear blurry. Yet, I was always there watching you, longing for you to see and come to Me.

When I look at you, I see you through My eyes of love. You are and always have been beautiful to Me. My love does not change when you fail or forget Me. It does not alter when you purposely walk away from what you know is right.

I look at your heart. And I wait for you to turn back to Me, for I am the One who knows the longing of your soul.

Do not see Me as a mere man who brings pain. I bring healing and hope. There is a future for you. All is not lost, for I am a God of second, third, and fourth chances. I care about what concerns you.

There is nothing good that I will withhold from you. Come to Me and let us reason together. I wish to give you the love you never had.

"I have loved you with an everlasting love. With lovingkindness I have drawn you."
Jeremiah 31:3

You will not always hurt

You will not always be in pain. Your heart will not always break. I died so your heart can be whole, and it shall be. Look to Me when you are alone and feel it will never change. There is love and companionship for you too. You are lovely to Me and to others.

The enemy of your soul wants you to stay in the past and relive the happy times of yesterday. But I point you towards tomorrow, for there is a future and a hope for you.

All things are possible in Me. I have joys waiting for you, but you must seek Me first. When you know Me, you will experience the source of all love. I will show you how to love when you do not feel like loving. I will show you compassion when you have none to give.

Look to My heart first. Look to Me first. Do not try to get from others what can only come from Me. Fellowship with Me when you feel empty and alone, as though you cannot go on one more day.

I shall sustain you. I will fill you beyond what you could ever dream or imagine. My love never runs dry. It is your source when you feel used up and tired. My love will speak to you when you need to hear a voice of kindness and acceptance. Ask to hear clearer. Come near Me and let Me whisper words of love to you. Forget the past and look to what lies ahead.

"For I know the thoughts that I think toward you, says the Lord, thoughts of peace and not of evil, to give you a future and a hope. Then you will call upon Me and go and pray to Me, and I will listen to you. And you will seek Me and find Me when you search for Me with all your heart." Jeremiah 29:11-13

Find rest in Me

Come to Me and find rest. You are busy running here and there, exhausting yourself, while I wait for you to see Me and come. I can give your heart rest. There are many things in which you excel. Many want to learn from you and partake in service with you. They see you and long to be near you and discover your joy of service. But you are too busy to slow down and see them.

I have gifted you in many ways to reach many people.

My heart breaks when I see you becoming tired, wanting to quit. Look to Me and My strength. I have the perfect solution to what is weighing your heart down. I wish to use you to teach others who are getting started. I want you to come along beside them as a mentor and friend and speak words of encouragement to them.

I am pleased with your service to Me. I know that your work comes from a heart of love for the people I have put in your life. I wish to increase your depth and take you higher. It starts by going lower in downtime with Me.

Rest. Quiet yourself.

Hear and get instruction from My heart. Let Me bless you with more. I will provide others to help you with the cares of the blessings.

Learn to love the quietness and presence of My love, like a tranquil river flowing that waters you and all you touch. My love will transform your energy level when you serve Me.

"Martha, Martha," the Lord replied, "you are worried and upset about many things. But only one thing is necessary. Mary has chosen the good part, and it will not be taken away from her." Luke 10:41-42

I am the truth

I am the God of wisdom. I know you are hungry for more love, power, wisdom—all that is found in Me. I have put that hunger in you so that you would seek Me with all your heart.

You do not have to remain hungry. You can know Me more intensely and feed on My life.

I wish for your soul to soar in My love! I want to speak My words of love and truth to you directly. I am waiting for you to come to Me and receive it.

Limited truth is available from the teachers and counselors of this world. But know that all the truth comes from Me, for I am the author of truth.

Too much time absorbing the mindset of this world's ideology can make your heart lukewarm towards Me. I long that you be hot towards Me. No one likes cold food that should be hot or food that is hot that should be cold. When you partake of the wisdom of this world contrary to My wisdom, you stay hungry.

Come to Me and let Me feed you.

I am the Good Shepherd and know what you need. My love is beyond any other love. I have never left you, and I never will. I wish to have more of a place in your thoughts and actions. This deeper place happens when you absorb My words and come to know Me as the author of those words. I created you with a purpose in mind, and that will not change. You can turn to Me anytime and get back on the track I have for you. All is not lost.

"And you will seek Me and find Me when you search for Me with all your heart." Jeremiah 20:13

Your sorrow will end

Your sorrow will end. You do not weep alone, for I have taken note of each tear that falls. I was there each night you were up with grief, wondering about the future, crying out to Me, agonizing about the what ifs.

Even though your emotions felt so intense, your pain so deep, and it seemed that I was not near; I was extremely close.

I caught your tears in My heart. I held your hand as you tossed, turned, and wept into your pillow. I saw all and was there with you. I love you so much!

Emotions can be tricky. They can cause a person to feel like they are alone in their pain. That is not true, for I gave My life to be with you.

I have promised always to be there.

The truth is you will not always be sad. I will come to you and turn your sorrow into dancing. Winter gives way to spring and spring to summer.

Even if you cannot hear birds in the dark of winter, they still sing. Or see the sun because the curtains of your heart are drawn in sorrow; it still shines underneath the clouds. So, it is with Me. I am still there even if you do not see or hear Me. But you will see again, and you will hear again! This, too, shall pass.

You will dance with joy yet again. Come to Me. It is okay to be weak, for I make you strong. I do not say be strong apart from Me. But with Me, you remain secure. My love stays in good times and bad, sorrow and joy.

"Weeping may endure for a night, but joy cometh in the morning." Psalm 30:5b

I hear you crying

I hear your cry for healing. I am the God who heals you. Man has been granted wisdom from Me to heal, but I do not need modern medicine to perform My miracles. It is not wrong to seek the aid of a doctor but pray for whatever doctor or treatment is best. And I will direct you. Have faith that I can do the impossible.

Please do not give up on seeking Me. Many of the people in the Bible received their healing because they would not stop asking. I delighted in their faith! Know that I love you even when the manifestation of your healing seems to tarry. It is not wasted time but a time for you to press in and know Me more.

I have not forgotten you, so do not get discouraged and forget Me. I am about a relationship, longing for you to come to me when you feel weak and sad from the ongoing delay.

Come to Me and feel My love. All the pains and troubles of the physical body will pass, but your relationship with Me will never end. Seek Me first. I long to know you more intimately. I long to talk with you. I delight in the sound of your laughter. I love to see you smile.

I was there when the doctor's excellent report came and also when the awful news came. I am greater than any report of health or sickness. I always give a good account of your health, for I am the God of more than enough! More than enough healing for your body and mind.

By My stripes, you are healed! All pain of this life will pass, but I remain.

"For I am the Lord who heals you." Exodus 15:26b

I am in love with you

I, the Lord, am in love with you. I celebrate you. I love it when something funny makes you laugh. It is music to My ears! Never does a moment go by that you are not on My mind and in My heart. Your beauty is always before Me, and I rejoice over you with singing. When you close your eyes at night, I stay to watch, giving you peace, caressing your heart and mind with my constant presence.

Others in your life may have left. New people may come, but I am forever constant. Never will I leave you. When your heart aches, I am there aching with you, whispering to you that this too shall pass. I am reminding you that you will laugh again.

When you are filled with happiness, I am also happy that you enjoy the life I have given you. I have more life, power, peace, and joy to bring to you.

My love for you cannot be exhausted. There is always plenty to spare! There is nothing that you could ever do that would change My heart towards you. If you have made mistakes, know I am ready to forgive and begin again.

I hope for an unbroken fellowship with you on your good and bad days. If there are times when you feel tired and weak, I stay, comforting you. Never will I leave you all alone when you feel sad, and tears fall.

I say to you, "Come away, My beautiful bride!
Come with Me and let Me show you how deep

and high My love for you is." Song of Solomon 2:10

I know you

My precious daughter, I knew and loved you before you knew yourself. I did not throw your life together in a chaotic, thoughtless fashion, but I carefully chose and molded each lovely part of you to become the person you are today. I created you in love. I thought of you before you came to be.

You are more precious to Me than the sun, moon, and stars that shine in the sky. You are lovelier to Me than the birds that sweetly sing. Or the many creatures that creep upon the ground.

Mountains are glorious and majestic. Many travel to them to refresh their souls and gain perspective on life. My love for you is higher than the highest mountain!

The roaring waters of the world bring exhilaration and refreshment in their splendor. Yet, their displayed power does not compare to the depth and intensity of My love for you.

So great is My love that not even death is strong enough to keep Me from you. I willingly gave My life so that you could be with Me forever. Do not doubt your worth. But even if you do, I will take all of eternity and show you how deep My love is for you.

It is finished! My love for you is sealed in My heart. You belong to Me. Rejoice in that love. Let it heal and strengthen—reminding you that you have a home, a father, and a husband. And we shall be together for always.

"Place me like a seal over your heart, like a seal on your arm; for love is as strong as death...Many waters cannot quench love; rivers cannot wash it away." Song of Songs 8:6 - 7

I give you rest

My lovely daughter, I know the anxiety that weighs you down, the stress and worries you have when you feel you cannot change or control events.

I am greater than all that troubles you. Even though the going can get rough, know that I am nearer to you when you need it the most.

Rest in Me.

Breathe in My presence.

I speak peace to your soul.

I have not asked you to change things that you cannot change. But to ask Me what I would have you do in any troubling situation. Never would I ask you to do something without supplying the strength you need.

I have not given you a spirit of weakness and fear but of boldness and power. I would not ask you to be bold if I knew you could not be brave.

I ask you to do things you feel you cannot do, so My power will be great in your weakness. I have given you a spirit of a sound and confident mind. You can do all things through Me. Ask for what you need.

I love you. And wait to fill you with more of Me. My love for you is settled. It is assured and does not change. The things you wish to do for Me are things I want to grow in you so that you can do them for My glory. My love is forever there, giving you all you need.

"For God did not give us a spirit of timidity, but a spirit of power, of love, and of self-discipline." 1 Timothy 1:7

My love just is

My lovely child, you cannot earn My love. My love just is. It is there when you wake and greet a new day. It is there when you close your eyes to sleep.

My love is constant when you are having a good day. And still there when you are having a grueling day. There is not one thing you can do to change how I feel about you.

I know you have at times not felt like you deserve My love. But I have always looked at you and saw a soul worthy of redemption, a child I longed to bless with an eternal home.

I am your perfect Father. You will not always understand My ways; they are higher than yours.

You have a special place at My table. There is a chair with your name, a place card that belongs to you only. Nobody can fill the spot at My table reserved just for you. Even when you feel like a failure, I do not take your place away and give it to another. It is for you alone.

I long for you. I long to see your face at my table, eating and drinking with me. I have a lovely garment of white for you to wear. It is your perfect size, and I wait expectingly to show it to you!

You are mine! My heart is yours! Rejoice, my daughter. Much joy awaits you in My Kingdom. Until then and for always, I am breathless with love for you, My beautiful daughter.

"How great is the love the Father has lavished on us, that we should be called children of God!" 1 John 3:1

I have not forgotten you

Though you may have felt forgotten by others, I cannot forget you. Your face is always before Me. I remember you when you are awake and doing busy things throughout the day. I see you sleep at night.

I know the things that break your heart. I see the sadness you feel when you feel forgotten by people in your life that matter to you. I draw close to you at those times.

Can you see Me there with you? Ask to see, and I will show you.

I do not love you more when you do an act of love for Me. I am glorified when you take My love to others in word and deed. But what you do does not decide whether I love you or not.

My love just is, and there is nothing you can do to change that. It is settled forever. Call Me when you feel alone and forgotten and let Me show you.

You will see and know it on the cool breeze that comes to you on a sweltering summer day. Or a hot cup of hot chocolate on a winter day enjoyed with a friend who seemed to visit on a whim. Or a new pet that needs you as much as you need him.

There was no chance these things happened to you when you needed them most. Ask Me to show you how I love you, and I will come quickly to your side.

I have not forgotten you, and I never will.

"Can a woman forget her nursing child and have no compassion on the son of her womb? Even these may forget, but I will not forget you. Behold, I have inscribed you on the palms of My hands; Your walls are continually before Me." Isaiah 49:15-16

Forever I will love you

How long is forever? Marriage between a man and woman is meant to last forever, but sometimes for various reasons, it does not.

My marriage to you is forever. No one can take you away from Me. Our union is permanently settled in Heaven.

When a man and woman union is formed, they become one in Spirit. The ripping apart of this union brings pain. I can heal that pain and restore joy once again.

Humans can, at times, love imperfectly. But I love perfectly. All it takes is one word, one touch from Me, and you can be whole again. I do not condemn, but I draw near you to heal you.

I see the hidden part of the heart that needs restoration.

My love is calling you to come; come and know the love that will not end. Other attachments may have hurt you; I am the love that will heal that hurt. Other people may have abandoned you; I am the love that will never leave you. Other relationships may have left you to cry alone; I am the love that will stay and dry those tears.

My great heart beats for you. I wish to reveal more of My love to you so that you will be confident and sure in that love.

I am drawing you to Myself. Do not fight it; embrace it, for it is good. You will not regret giving your all to Me.

I am a dependable God. From everlasting to everlasting, My love will be faithful.

"I have loved you with an everlasting love;
Therefore, with lovingkindness I have drawn
you and continued My faithfulness to you."
Jeremiah 31:3

I did not make a mistake in creating you

Like chocolate in a candy mold, I am molding and making you to be like Me. I love you as you are right this moment. That will not change. But I also see what you can become.

I see what you want to be. You have asked Me to make you more like Me, and I shall do that. I know the exact ingredients to put in the mold. All I do is done in love with thought for your future. With the finished product in mind, I carefully added the needed parts.

Some chocolate is sweeter and made with more sugar. Other kinds have unique flavors and fruits like coconut, peanut butter, or nuts. Some varieties are darker with little milk added, and some with a lot of cream.

All that I create is wonderful and perfect. I make no mistakes when I create, even though the mixing may look chaotic.

At times, the blending and molding can feel painful. But you are kept safe and secure as you abide in My love. If you listen carefully, you will hear My voice speaking words of comfort and instruction.

I have much planned for you!

Everyone likes to open a box of chocolates in a pretty heart-shaped container. Likewise, you are in My heart. And you shall be used for My purpose to bring much joy to others.

I am making you with love. The best is yet to come! Abide in Me as I abide in you, and you will have all you need.

"Abide in Me, and I will abide in you. Just as the branch cannot produce fruit by itself unless it abides in the vine, neither can you unless you abide in Me." John 15:4

I know you are tired

I know the winter has been long. I know your heart is tired. I also am aware that this season of sadness will pass. You shall laugh again. In the very depth of the sorrow, I am present. Never was there a moment when you were all alone, even though you may have felt that you were. I understand the need you have for solitude. I, too, needed to be alone with My father when I walked the earth.

There is no solitude of the soul that I do not know. I come when you need it the most. I give you the strength to continue. As I have helped you in the past, I will continue to help you be strong, to go on. I give hope when it seems to have flown away. I am hope. And you have Me constantly, so you always have hope. You can sing for I am your song in the night. You can laugh, for I have defeated all that is against you.

You can sleep in peace, for I give you rest and set My angels about you to protect you in all your ways. You can dream, for I give you dreams to dream when the old ones have died. It is always springtime in Me. Always there is life after death.

You can be confident, for I am your confidence in times of uncertainty. Never will I leave you. Come, let us go and smell the sweet fragrance of the flowers I planted just for you.

"My beloved spoke and said to me, "Arise, my darling, my beautiful one, come with me. See!

The winter is past; the rains are over and gone. Flowers appear on the earth; the season of singing has come; the cooing of doves is heard in our land. The fig tree forms its early fruit; the blossoming vines spread their fragrance. Arise, my darling, my beautiful one, come with me." Song of Songs 2:10-13

I bring refreshment to your soul

My dear daughter, I know the sacrifice's you made to bring My love to others. My heart swells with pride when I see all you have done for Me; how you spoke My name when it was not popular. How you chose to love when it was hard, not expecting anything in return. I am pleased that you have held My name high and glorified Me. Come to Me now and find rest for your soul. I can see you are weary. I want to refresh you with My presence.

The battle has been intense, and you have stood firm. Let Me show you how precious you are to Me. I have good things prepared for you. Not a moment goes by when I do not think of you and how much I love you. I have loved you with My life. I want to continually feed you My life so you might live in abundance.

I know when you thirst, and I have drink from My heart for you. I know when you hunger and can find nothing to satisfy; let Me help you. I am your hunger and your satiation. I have good food for you at My table. Come and dine! Come and lie your head on My breast. I shall soothe all that troubles you.

The battles have been fierce, but I have already won them. As I took care of you yesterday, so shall I take care of you today and tomorrow. Do not fret! Do not worry! Only stop all striving and come to Me and find rest. You do not have to earn your salvation. I had done that already when I called you and laid down My life for you. No greater love will you ever find than the love that I love you with today, tomorrow, and forever.

"Greater love has no one than this than to lay down his life for his friends." John 15:13

I come to you

My beautiful daughter, when your pain is deep and you feel all alone in the depth of your soul with no song to sing, I come and sing to you of My love.

There is no depth of sorrow, failure, no darkness, piercing pain of soul, or unrelenting pain of body that I am not deeper than.

I can penetrate the blackest darkness and bring light. I hear the faintest cry for help from you, My child, and come when you call.

I can light up the darkest hole on earth and rescue from the most bottomless pit.

There is no darkness that I am not deeper than. I see you when you feel that you are invisible.

I hear you when you feel that you have lost your voice. I stay with you when you think that all have left.

Do you know that I cannot stop loving you? Do you know that you cannot exhaust the supply of My love? Like a gushing waterfall that does not end, there is enough of My love to fill the world repeatedly.

Sing, for I am near. Breathe deep, for I am with you.

All pain and trouble of this life will end, and you will be with Me forever. Sing, My lovely daughter, sing of My love for you. And I will listen and smile with joy at the sound.

"Deep calls to deep in the roar of your waterfalls; all your waves and breakers have swept over me. By day, the Lord directs his love, at night his song is with me - a prayer to the God of my life." Psalm 42:7-8

I am lasting beauty

My child, I know it is easy to get caught up in the buying and selling of material things of this passing world. But understand that this is not where your real peace and joy are found.

Lasting contentment comes from knowing Me. I am the foundation you need. Look to Me to find lasting beauty. It is not wrong to wish to be surrounded by lovely things if I am at the center. And in your happiness, you remember to give to others.

Fellowship with Me, and I will show you all I have stored up for you. Much stress can come with the keeping of temporary treasures of this world. But the treasures you store with Me are kept safe, and nothing can destroy them.

See My handiwork in the heavens above! Hear My voice in the bubbling creek. See My beauty in the fresh white snow that falls. Or the cool rain that I send on scorching summer days.

I have laid up a foundation of beauty and pleasure that far surpasses all you can now see and know. Seek Me. And you shall know, for I wish to show you the good things that are still to come.

There is music ready to sound that you have not heard. There are sights in the heavens ready to be displayed you have not seen. There are myriad textures and colors, rare gems and mountains and waters, and so much more that I have stored up for your pleasure. Enjoy the many wonders of this world but always remember the best is coming. And it is no loss to give what you have to others, so they too can know the treasure in Me.

"You afflicted, tossed with storms, and not comforted, behold, I will set your stones in beautiful colors, and lay your foundations with sapphires." Isaiah 54:11

Always I have loved you

Sometimes it is easy to love. Sometimes it is not. But if you ask for the love I can pour into you, you will have more than enough.

I do not ask you to give water to the thirsty when your well is dry. You must come to Me and drink until your thirst is satisfied.

I do not ask you to give what you do not have.

My love is perfect, and it covers a multitude of sins. If all you can see when you greet a sibling is their sin that they have confessed, then come to Me. I will show you how I have covered and forgiven them.

Then it will be easier to love, as I love you.

How have I loved you?

Before you knew Me, I loved you.

Before you came to Me, I loved you while you were still in sin.

When you were in rebellion, not caring who you hurt, I loved and called you back home to Me. And like the prodigal son, I was instructing My servants to prepare the fatted calf for soon you shall return, and we shall celebrate.

You did not choose Me, but I chose you.

Come to Me, and I will show you how high, comprehensive, and deep My love is. Let it change you and make you like Me. I command you to love. But I do not expect you to do it without Me. I am love. I can love the unlovely and lovely alike. And you can too when you love as I love with My Spirit in you.

"This is My commandment, that you love one another as I have loved you." John 15:12

Morning kisses

You may think you have found Me, but I was never far from you, My sweet love. I always had you in My heart. When you woke feeling tired this morning and did not want to get up, I loved you and was busy preparing blessings for you.

I have set a breakfast of mercy for My mercies are new every morning. A warm bath has been drawn so you can bathe in My peace. And so, you can know the cleansing and empowering strength I give as you rest in Me, soaking in My presence.

As you dress and think about your day, I am there helping you prioritize. You do not walk alone into a new day, for I am present, waiting for you, ready to take you where you need to go—hoping we can often talk throughout the day.

I liked your idea to stop and get foil-wrapped candy kisses to share with your co-workers to sweeten their day. I, too, have special kisses wrapped just for you—in the sunshine that will warm your face on this cold winter day.

Kisses are coming in the project that will finally come together, and along the way, when you help the old gentleman reach a jar of peanut butter at the grocery store, and when you stop to listen to him talk about his day. I kissed you when you gave a sweet smile and words of encouragement to the stressed-out checker at the store. And again, when you let that car go before you as you waited in a line of traffic.

It is more blessed to give than to receive. And I will continue to love and bless the one My heart has always loved.

"I have found the one my heart loves." Song of Songs 3:4

My love is perfect

My beautiful Bride, I have come for you not because you are perfect but because My love for you is perfect. When you confess your sins to Me, all is forgiven, and I remember your sins no more.

Before you came to Me, I came to you.

I do not regret pouring out My love to you.

I did not regret it when I hung on the cross for your salvation.

I do not regret that sacrifice today when I see you.

I know the enemy comes and tells you that all is lost, that you have messed up again and did the same old sin. He torments you and says you are a failure and not even your Creator can help you now. That is a lie! No one is beyond My reach.

Reach to Me and take My hands that are outstretched still.

Come now and let us reason together. Though your sins are like scarlet, they shall be as white as snow; Though they are red like crimson, they shall be as wool. (Isaiah 1:18)

My hands are hands that heal.

Some hands hurt, but My hands are more prominent than those hands. They are filled with gentle love for you. Receive it. It is for you too.

I long to heal, restore, and show you all the good things I have in store for you. Come. I am still waiting for you. Stay with Me until you feel the old passing away and new strength and vision come to you. It will change you and help you to be what you have always wanted to be in Me.

"God shows his love for us in that while we were still sinners, Christ died for us." Romans 5:8

The prison door is open

My lovely one, I see how you have beat against the prison bars that you think are still there. But I have set you free. You can now walk into the next place I have for you.

No tears will be wasted. No struggle that you had and overcame in Me will go without it being used for good in your life and the lives of others. But first, you must realize who I am and what I have done for you.

When I died upon the cross, My eyes were on you. I knew what you would need. And where you would be and the thoughts you would be thinking. I knew the pain you would feel and how you felt like it would never end. I also saw the victory coming to you when you called out to Me. Even when you did not know it was Me you were calling for, your spirit knew, and I set in motion My power and deliverance to come to you. I arranged for people to come into your life who would help you.

Look up from where you sit and see Me. I am there holding the doors open for you. I will wait for you to come. It does not matter where you are or what you are doing. I am the One who has come to set you free inside. And then you shall go out and tell of all My wondrous deeds.

Dry your tears and look up. See Me in the kind words from the helpers I sent to you. And in the very words, I spoke for you in My word. Come, My Bride, the prison door is open.

"The Spirit of the Lord GOD is upon me, because the LORD has anointed me to bring good news to the afflicted; He has sent me to bind up the brokenhearted, to proclaim liberty to captives and freedom to prisoners." Isaiah 61:1

My love burns for you

My wonderful Bride, My love is a fire that has no end.

It is an extravagant love that no other love can come close to or understand. I loved the world and proved it by giving My only son. And I still love the world today. No human can start this fire, for it comes from the depth of My heart. But humans can invite the fire of My love and keep it burning.

I see how you have warmed yourself in the fire of My love. And how you have given that love away. I am pleased with your sacrifice. Know that there is enough fire to keep all warm.

There is an adequate fire of love to stay burning throughout all eternity. Natural fires are put out with water but not the fire of My passion. No water can quench it. No floods of tragedy or disaster, manufactured or natural, can stop My love from burning.

Sometimes you may feel like you have only a tiny spark of My love. That is all you need, for My love grows when My Spirit brings life into that spark. I can make the most minor and driest log burn brightly. And I can make a wet, tear-soaked log spark and light up and warm a whole city.

I am the source of all love, the source of all energy. Have faith in what I can do through you. All it takes is a willing heart, laying down who you are, and taking up who I am. This action will light and warm your way and show the way for others who will come after you.

Come, My love, and feel the heat of My love. I will speak fiery light into your darkness. And fuel your heart with abundant love and hope.

"Many waters cannot quench love, neither can the floods drown it." Song of Songs 8:7

It is okay to need Me

My lovely one, you are not wrong to need to lean on Me.

I know that you are weary from the battle. I am your strength.

You lose no time when you are with Me in the wilderness of My love. That is where you find out who you are by finding out who I am. It is away from all human activity and voices where you can hear My voice. This is where you see Me through eyes unhindered.

Freely speak of your pain. Show Me where it hurts.

I love to hear you speak!

I love to be so close to you that I feel your heartbeat with Mine.

You lose no time on the battlefield when you rest to soak in My love. My love is the strategy you need to go and fight the good fight and win.

You are not weak if you need Me. But instead, you become ineffective if you say you do not need Me.

The wilderness of My love is vast. I loved you through every phase of your journey, even when you did not want Me there.

I loved when you turned away. And I loved you when you returned. I did not move away but stayed near you, watching you, hoping you would turn to Me again and let Me love you.

You were made to need Me. My love is wide enough to take in all of who you are today and tomorrow. I will wait for you to learn to love to lean on Me. I wait for you to come to know the completeness in Me as your lover, Creator, and God.

"Who is this coming up from the wilderness, leaning on her beloved?" Song of Songs 8:5

I know the heartache in dealing with people

I understand the struggle in loving the unlovely. I know how it feels when those close to you become your enemies.

I can supernaturally give you the grace to love the unlovely. I, too, had close friends who betrayed Me when I walked the earth. And it hurt.

I loved the world so much that I gave My life so that you could know eternal life.

I love all the people in the world, not just the ones who would love Me back. I died for sinners: all people, even those who perform ungodly acts, causing horrible pain to humanity.

My love does not change. From the cross, I cried, "Father forgive them, for they know not what they do." The fallen, sinful man in them is offending you when someone hurts you. Indeed, they do not know what they do. They can only be loving like Me when they, with My power, come to Me and take on My nature. Not all know this power is available to them or how to obtain it.

Go and love, My Bride. I love the unlovely. Give, lend, not expecting them to return the favor. And I shall reward you.

You reflect Me, and I am love. Love all with a pure love that is not based on performance. With My power in you, you can love as I love.

"But love your enemies, do good, and lend, hoping for nothing in return; and your

---

reward will be great, and you will be sons of the Highest. For He is kind to the unthankful and evil. Therefore, be merciful, just as your Father also is merciful." Luke 6:35

You are not alone in your pain

My beautiful Bride, you are not alone in your pain. I know your heart hurts. I am the God who heals.

I am the strong tower that you can run to and find safety. When the winds of change blow on you, and you feel alone and exposed to the elements; I remain.

You do not sleep alone. You do not wake alone.

You may feel strong emotions when night falls, and the memories come flooding back. Know that I am with you at those times. I come close and comfort you.

I am closer than the very air you breathe. I am nearer to you when you need Me. Long ago, you asked Me to come and never leave, and I said yes. My yes is not dependent upon your performance or mood. My yes is based on My love for you, which cannot change.

Intense winds blow in life. And you have known many. Please remember that I have been where you are; I have felt the same loneliness that you feel.

I will not leave you all alone. The storm is not greater than My love. The winds are not able to uproot My presence. No rain can wash away My promise to always be with you. No one can snatch you out of My hand. No eternal harm can ever come to you, for you are grounded in Me.

Be of good cheer! The one who loves you most is with you today. I will heal your heart and bind up your wounds.

Rest in My Love. Close your eyes and rest. All is well. You are safe with Me.

"He heals the brokenhearted and binds up their wounds." Psalm 147:3

I hear your cry

A river of love is flowing to you. No more will your life feel arid and empty. I, the Lord, hear your cry. And I am coming. You belong to Me. I bought you at a price. I am a jealous God. I will not allow the enemy of your soul to give you food that will not satisfy you. Or drink that will not quench your thirst. I am your Maker and know what you need. I loved you before the foundations of the world were laid.

I planned each day of your life. I rejoiced the day your life formed, and you took your first breath. You are perfect! —the beautiful hairs on your head, the color of your eyes, the shape of your mouth, and the very essence of who you are fills Me with eternal love!

I have called you and given you all you need for life. You belong to Me. I know the enemy has tried to tell you that you are worthless and have made too many mistakes. He lied to you and said I have stopped loving you.

Never can I stop loving you! Your face is engraved on the palm of my hand. It is always before Me, and I say that it is good. I do not look at your failures. Whether you succeed or fail, you will always be in the center of My heart. I can make you stand firm and victorious. I am Your help. Troubles shall not shake you because I am your sure foundation.

Come, let us reason together and begin again. Come, My lovely Bride. I will wait for you, and you will bathe in the river of My love and life.

"There is a river whose streams make glad the city of God, the holy dwelling places of the Most High. God is in the midst of her, and she will not be moved; God will help her when morning dawns." Psalm 46: 4-5

You belong

My Bride, you belong. You are not an abandoned orphan. You have a forever home in Me. I know you have been hurt by those who were supposed to love and care for you.

I will pick you up, hold you, and fill all the holes in your heart. You are My child.

You are adopted into My family and take My name. I have always loved you. But I do not force anyone to accept My love. I want a soul to choose to come to Me, allowing Me to love and heal them.

You have cried out to Me for answers, for healing. I am here as you asked.

You will forget the pain of your past. No longer will you be called forsaken and fatherless. You belong to Me! You are welcome to have all that is Mine as My child. There is so much I long to show you and give to you! We shall be together forever. Our love relationship will never end.

Do not look in empty wells for that only found in Me. I will quench your thirst. I am there to satisfy the hunger in the depth of your heart.

My beautiful love, you are no longer a slave. You shall no longer fear, for I have set a place for you at My table as My child—a love birthed in My heart.

There is no one like Me. And there is no one like you.

We belong together. Let us break bread together and talk of wonders yet to come.

"For you did not receive a spirit that makes you a slave again to fear, but you received the Spirit of sonship. And by Him we cry, `Abba, Father.'" Romans 8:15

The battle is Mine

My beautiful Bride, I know it can be hard to be silent when someone has been unkind to you. I appreciate you exercising self-control and not getting defensive.

Not all know Me as you know Me.

Not all have experienced My love. Everyone does not know My heart that holds all things together. Thank you for the times you kept silent when words would have started an uncontrollable wildfire. Many battles are not yours to fight. I, who see and hear everything, will even the score in the end. I only ask you to walk in My love. Live in peace as much as you are able.

When the tension has passed, your silence will have spoken louder than anger.

Only My love in you can give you the strength to not speak. My love constrains you when you are tempted to say something that could cause harm. Remember when I was accused, I spoke not a word to My accusers. This is not to say that you never speak up, but there are many times when speaking would not help, and silence is better served.

Seek Me. Get your directions from the Holy Spirit, who is always with you. Bring the fruit of self-control to those who have no self-control. Practice the fruit of My Spirit, and you will be blessed and live in harmony with those around you. A gentle answer turns away wrath. Bring My love and peace through your words *and* your silence.

"For the love of Christ constrains us." 1 Corinthians 5:15

You are beautiful to Me

I bought you, My dear one, with My life; you are beautiful to Me. And always will be.

My heart is in you, and your heart is in Me.

No love can compare to My love for you. You are precious and lovely to behold. That is the final word—no other opinion matters. I understand there are standards of beauty in the world. I know how easy it is to compare yourself to those standards. However, I do not compare you to anyone else. In My eyes, you are altogether lovely. No hard day when you feel less than your best can change that. No time when you might act in a way that is not pleasing can vary how I have decided to think about you for all eternity.

The world will never see you as I see you.

The world will never love you as I love you.

You are perfect in My sight. And I call you worthy for you are fearfully and wonderfully made. I was there in the beginning when you were formed in your mother's womb. I rejoiced the day you were born.

As a rose is still a rose and incredibly beautiful no matter what vase it might be in, so too are you. I created you, and I do not make mistakes even if others may have called you a mistake.

Even if you keep messing up, I still see beauty and perfection. See yourself as I see you. Ask Me to help you see through My eyes, and then you shall see clearly.

Marvelous are My works, and you are My best work.

"I will praise You, for I am fearfully and wonderfully made; Marvelous are Your works, and that my soul knows very well." Psalm 139:14

I will quiet you in My love

My dear one, I am your peace when your heart is disturbed. I know the ways this world can rock your world making you feel lost and alone at sea. I understand how storms can make you feel like there is no solid ground.

I long to be your peace in storms like a mother bird who protects her young under the shelter of her wings. I want you to see the wind and the rain as signals to go deeper into Me where there is safety. Where all you can hear while the storm rages all around you is My voice of love, quieting you, singing gently to you,

"Peace. Peace. Be still. All is well. I am with you."

I understand the time's trouble was so great and your pain so intense that you prayed for Me to take you home. I have given you a job to do in this world for My glory. Until that is complete, you will have the grace you need to remain and be faithful.

With Me, you can sing in the storm, for I am your shelter. You can rest in the boat rocking in the stormy waves, for I am your anchor. I am in the storm because you are there. I love you and will never leave you. Ask Me to show you where I am when trouble comes your way, and you will see with new eyes.

And on that final homecoming day, when your boat arrives safely on Heaven's shore, I will rejoice over you with loud singing. You will be glad you trusted Me to navigate till the end of the journey.

"The LORD, your God, is in your midst, a mighty One who will save; he will rejoice over you with gladness; He will quiet you by his love; He will exult over you with loud singing."
Zephaniah 3:17

I loved you first

My precious Bride, I see you long to be near Me and hear My heart. Wonderful! But know, I loved you first before you even stepped towards Me. I know you cannot find Me without Me showing you the way and putting the map in your heart.

I cannot love you more by you striving to try and earn My love through your good works. I love you already! Right this moment. Exactly where you are, even if you do not acknowledge Me. Even if you purposely sinned and forgot that you belong to Me.

It can be hard to imagine such a love as this, but it exists. And it is how I love you. I loved the men who put Me on the cross and the ones who cursed My name. I loved the men who nailed Me to the tree and the men who spat on Me. I loved those who called Me a liar and said I had a demon. I loved the men who said I did not speak the words of My Father and the men who betrayed Me. I loved the ones who sold Me, the people who turned back from following Me, and those who only followed Me to get something from Me. I loved those who did not love Me but only sought to kill Me and then lie about My resurrection.

I loved them all though they hated Me. So, you see, there is nothing you can do to make Me not love you. Come to Me as you are and know this unconditional love is for you.

Listen, for My love is calling to you still. Answer yes, and let this love live through you.

"In this, the love of God was made manifest among us, that God sent His only Son into the world, so that we might live through Him. In this is love, not that we have loved God but that He loved us...." I John 4:9-10

I am your hope

My chosen one, I long to give you hope and a constant stream of peaceful assurance. There is a place of safety in Me where you can abide. It is a lovely place where you live in fellowship with Me, and My Spirit speaks to you. Outside of Me, hope is short-lived and futile.

My hope is fueled by genuine love. Seek Me in the silence of your soul, and you will find Me. My love will come to you in the fullness you need. Rest in Me and wait to hear My still, small voice.

Take the time to get to know the sound of Me. You need not fear that I will give you hope and then dash that hope on the rocks of past failures and fears.

I speak the truth, not lies. You can trust My heart of love to give you what you need.

Sometimes I will tell you to stop, look and proceed slowly.

Or I will say, slow down and turn around now, for there is danger up ahead!

And I might say, go now. I have prepared the way, and this is of Me.

Or rest my beautiful one. Let Me heal your wounds and make you whole again.

I bring you hope fueled with love. Trust Me with your future. Listen, and you shall eat the good fruit of the land I am leading you to, with no shame or regret.

"Hope does not put us to shame because God's love has been poured into our hearts through the Holy Spirit who has been given to us."
Romans 5:5

You are from My heart

You belong with Me, My child. At times, it appeared like you had no place or foundation.

I know that life has hurt you. It has made you feel like an orphan. Even the most loving human being still loves imperfectly at times.

But all the kindness you have experienced, the times you felt loved and appreciated, if only for a moment, was from Me reaching out to you.

I can heal the holes that others have left in your heart.

I can fill them in so well that you will not even know where the original crack was.

It is not too late to begin again.

Come to Me. Let us talk about the early days when the wound first appeared. I can show you My love in that area, so it has no more power over you.

I can give you the strength you need to walk away from the things of darkness that keep that original hurt alive. I can root out the bad seed and plant new seed into the ground that has been called desolate.

My eyes are on you for good! Not to condemn you, but to save you and heal you.

"See what kind of love the Father has given to us, that we should be called children of God; and so, we are." 1 John 3:1

My love covers all

My love, I love all. I do not only love those who have done virtuous deeds and spoken kind words to others but also those who are far from Me in thought and deed.

I love those who hate Me. My love is not like the love of many people in this world—love that loves someone if they are like themselves.

I love all people! The person who seeks Me, changes, and does good things. And I love the person who does not desire me—the one who continues to do bad things, harming themselves and others.

There is no love like Mine.

With this kind of love, the world can be turned upside down! I know you know this kind of love. But many do not.

My love is the kind of love that grows when it is given away. It is not meant to stay confined to a church building or a home. It needs wings that will fly to forsaken places. And give hope to those who have not heard the Good News.

If you want greater joy, then go and be My wings. Give out of the abundance I have given you. I love you so much!

Trust Me. You will have all you need. Nothing will be impossible for you, for I am with you. I shall fill you with more love as you give away love to those who have none. You shall be filled with joy when you see My love on the faces of those who are lonely and lost.

Go, My love and in My name show My heart that loves the sinner. My love came so they could have eternal life in Me.

"God shows his love for us in that while we were still sinners, Christ died for us." Romans 5:8

Ask Me for clarity

My dear one, trouble cannot keep Me from you. Struggles can be intense. They can cause you to see and feel things not of Me. Ask Me for clarity.

There is no power as strong as the power of My love.

Death may seem more potent, but it is not, for I conquered death. It is under My feet. Temptations in this life cannot stop the flow of My love.

The enemy's plan is for you to fall and deny Me by your actions and words. But His plans are not strong enough to eradicate My plan. You are more than a conqueror through Me. Nothing created nothing above or below, is more significant than Me. Come to Me and let Me show you.

All trouble of this life passes. Press into Me when you feel pressure to give up or give in. Stay with Me. And you shall be made strong.

If the time ever comes when grief or trouble is so great that you have no strength to pray, say My name. And I will carry you. It is not by might or power but by My Spirit that shall bring victory. My angels are at My command. You will not be alone.

My love is more significant than hate. You will reign with Me forever, My beautiful Bride.

"In all these things, we are more than conquerors through Him who loved us. For I

am sure that neither death nor life, nor angels nor rulers, nor things present nor things to come, nor powers, nor height nor depth, nor anything else in all creation, will be able to separate us from the love of God in Christ Jesus our Lord." Roman's 8:37-39

I know your needs

My dear one, I have made a way for you to come to Me—to approach Me without fear.

I am a God of compassion and anticipate your every need. And I will have mercy upon you, for I love you with an everlasting love. Come to Me with all that troubles your heart today. Do not hold back.

I know all and see all. You can talk to Me about anything, and I will listen. I made you! I gave My life to you. You need not be ashamed of your weakness. I can help you to be strong and overcome.

See My faithfulness all around you in the smiles of people who care about you. That is from Me.

Trust Me with the things you do not understand. Trust that I will be there tomorrow and help you as I have been your aid in the past. Others may have left you when you needed them, but I will never leave you.

Your future is complete!

I know it is hard to let go of yesterday. With Me, you need not worry about tomorrow, for I am already there. I know the meaning behind your every sigh. I know the things that make you laugh and fill you with joy. I did not rebuke Moses for desiring to be closer to Me, to know Me better. And I will not rebuke anyone now who wants to know Me more.

Come and know Me. You will discover how compassionate and loving I am, slow to anger and merciful.

The LORD passed in front of Moses, calling out,
"Yahweh! The LORD! The God of compassion
and mercy! I am slow to anger and filled with
unfailing love and faithfulness." Exodus 34:6

I understand your loss

My child, I know seeing good things in your future is hard.

I know you longed for the past when your days were happy, before the illness, before your kids left home when your husband was alive. I know.

Change and endings can be challenging. The good news is, I never change!

I was there when you felt that life was perfect when your children were small and close to you when you had excellent health and enough money to pay your bills.

Life in the body is complex. But there is hope! Because I change not and am all-powerful and all-knowing, I can also renew your spirit.

I can give life to the part that lives forever as you wait for the newness of your body. It is the longing of all humanity to have a body that does not wear out. To be at peace and have enough of everything necessary for life. When there is any lack or waiting time, I come and comfort you.

I direct you to My word, where you can read the truth of what I have planned for you. Man cannot find the contentment they long for apart from Me. I created man, and I know what it takes to be happy, to survive.

My mercies, My compassions never ended. I know the way of mankind. I am there to direct into endless abundance. Come to Me and have hope for who I am!

Come and know Me, ask, listen, and live. Experience My love, and you will see and experience eternal life.

When I rose from the dead, I appeared to My disciples on the shore, asking them, "Children, do you have any fish?" When they said that they did not, I supplied. I shall do the same for you in all areas of need.

Come. Ask. And live.

"The steadfast love of the Lord never ceases;
His mercies never come to an end."
Lamentations 3:22

My love gives

My lovely one, My love gives. And I gave the best of My love to you

Because I first gave to man, man, in turn, can now give back to his fellow man and Me. You need not wait to desire to give. You need not give because your friend or neighbor first gave. You can give because you have My heart that loves all equally and gives abundantly.

I know that you have given of yourself to others.

I am pleased you have put others' needs above yours. But I also want to remind you to come to Me and fuel up before your tank drains.

I do not expect you to give when you are empty, exhausted to the point of illness. It would help if you learned to rest and know that it is okay to say no.

I realize that many need and depend on you. Ask Me for help, and I shall give you wisdom. You shall then be fresh and able to offer from a whole heart and a strong body. There are still ways to help when you are weak and waiting to be healed. You can pray for others, talk to Me, let Me love on you, and you can love on Me.

I am the God who gave and still gives to all today.

Give of yourself to Me, rest, and listen. And you will have more than enough to give to others.

"For God loved the world so much that he gave His one and only son so that everyone who believes in Him will not perish but have eternal life." John 3:16

Your roots go deep in Me

My Bride, you can experience My love even if you do not understand how it works.

You can know Me and My love even if there are times you wonder how I can still love you.

I am not looking for perfection but faithfulness to come to Me with all your heart.

If you have fallen into sin, let Me know.

Talk to Me if you are weak and want to give in.

If you are wondering why I did what I did or why I did not answer the way you wanted Me to answer, ask Me. I long for you to know Me. I only have your best in mind. I know that sometimes it does not feel like that, but it is true.

There can be many reasons why things did not go as you prayed. Seek Me, and I will give you wisdom and peace. I have not left you an orphan trying to find your way in a confusing world.

I am Your comfort in the storm. You belong! Each time you come to Me and read My word, asking for understanding, your roots go deeper in Me. You do not need to have all the answers for your Papa God does. Cry out to know My love that is deeper than deep. The winds of uncertainty and change shall not uproot you. You are forever complete in Me and My unchanging love.

"Then Christ will make His home in your hearts as you trust Him. Your roots will grow down

into God's love and keep you strong. And may you have the power to understand, as all God's people should, how wide, how long, how high, and how deep His love is. May you experience the love of Christ, though it is too great to understand fully. Then you will be made complete with all the fullness of life and power that comes from God." Ephesians 3:17-19

I know it can be hard to love

My precious child, I know it can be hard to love your sibling when you have disagreements. When you both feel your viewpoint is essential. But do not stop seeking to love each other. Then, the world will see how you treat each other and get a picture of how I love them. They will see Me in you.

I am pleased when you try to bring peace and love and agree to disagree on matters of contention. It is only through Me that true peace and love can be found, for I am the source.

You belong to Me, and that will not change. With that in mind, why does it matter if you must give in to another in brotherly or sisterly love? Why do you have to be right? I love you so much and want everyone to live in harmony. Thank you for trying to bring peace to the storms in your life. Thank you for loving Me when it has been challenging. I am grateful that you have taken My name and lifted it high in the face of controversy.

I will settle all the wrongs in time. The unredeemed will give an account of every idle word. Do not worry. Come to Me and take on My spirit of contentment.

Walk in love. Be love, and the world will see and give glory to Me. Through Me, this is possible, for I first loved you and will forever do so.

"So now I am giving you a new commandment: Love each other. Just as I have loved you, you should love each other. Your *love for one another will prove to the world that you are My disciples." John 13:34-35*

You shall see My glory

My lovely Bride, praise Me, for I am in control.

Worship Me, for I am with you and will never leave you. My love has no end. It will not break or bend or let you down. Sorrow can be intense, and then it lightens. Through it all, I remain.

Glorify Me, for My love is with you today! Ask for more of it. Seek to know Me better. And I will answer and show you great and mighty things. I enjoy it when My children ask to see it. I did not rebuke Moses for wanting to see My glory, and I will not condemn you. Moses was brave and faithful, but he was also a human like you.

Ask, and you shall receive!

Seek Me in My word. You can do nothing to stop My love from flowing towards you. All of eternity will not be enough time for you to see all that I have for you. And it is all because of love. Take this love without fear, and you shall know mighty miracles in My name. You have believed, and now you shall see the rewards of your faith by receiving what you have asked.

Give thanks and be confident in your God!

Go forth into the darkness carrying My light, for I am with you. I am your steadfast rock in a land of sinking sand. You will be safe with Me. Thank Me for my presence and provision, and go in My name, My love.

Give glory to Me, and you shall see My glory.

"Give thanks to the God of heaven, for His steadfast love endures forever." Psalm 136:26

Seek My plan

My lovely Bride, have your plans failed? You desired to know the future and organize your money and relationships, but it all backfired.

Come to Me and let Me show you what I have in store for you. There is only so much you can plan for in this world. And nothing is safe outside of Me.

I have laid up blessings for you and a crown of glory! Seek Me regarding your future and what I would have you do. One never knows when they will take their last breath on earth. And indeed, you can take nothing with you except Me and what you have done for My glory.

Seek Me and My plan. You will not be sorry. You can start anew right now. Give Me your heart and all you have accumulated. I do not ask everyone to sell everything and give to the poor, but I do ask some to do that.

Do not fear that I will take what you have and leave you with nothing. I never ask for something without giving something back in return. And what I give back is far better than anything in this passing world.

Seek Me. Specify what I would have you do. And you will have peace that passes your understanding. All I have planned for you is good! Look to store up riches in Heaven where it is kept safe with Me. I am a good Father who wants you to have many rewards. Hear Me calling you to abundant life today and for all eternity.

"For I know the thoughts that I think toward you, says the Lord, thoughts of peace and not of evil, to give you a future and a hope."
Jeremiah 29:11

I give you hope

My child, do not lose hope! I will do what seems impossible to you.

My riches are more extraordinary than anything you can imagine.

My love for you is endless. I am still working in your life. I have not quit. Trust Me.

The dreams that come from Me will be fulfilled. Any goals that would bring you or another harm need to be brought to Me. Because I understand you, I will help you and not condemn you.

I know the way has been long. I know you are tired of waiting. I am your strength when it feels that you cannot hold on one moment longer. Minute by minute, day by day, I come and help you.

I direct you even if you feel that you cannot see the next step. I will whisper to you to "Go this way," or "To the right," or "To the left." You will not miss it if you listen and obey. Even if you make a mistake, I will be there and help you get back on track.

A tree of life is coming for you! I have not forgotten you and the prayers you prayed for your entire life. When hope for the answered prayer is deferred, hang on, dear one. Only a little longer, and the answer will be there.

Come to Me and let Me comfort you. Know Me in the waiting time, and your love for Me will grow. You will see that I was in this all along. I always had your best in mind.

Come, My love, and let Me love you.

Rest in Me and trust Me. And I will guard Your heart and mind, preparing you for good things that are to come.

"Hope deferred makes the heart sick, but when the desire comes, it is a tree of life." Proverbs 13:12

I am near

My beautiful Bride, I hear you calling out to Me. And I am near.

Come and pray to Me.

Talk to Me in the quiet so you can hear My love softly coming to you like a gentle breeze.

I long to give you what you need. Seek Me with all your heart and ready yourself to receive My riches.

You have asked for a refreshing wave of cleansing water. It is coming. The passion of the fire of My glory is wanted. It is coming! I hear your every desire!

I know what your lonely sighs mean. I know the ache in your heart for more of Me.

I love you so much! I long to unleash more blessings on you. If you want more of Me, ask! I love it when you ask to know Me more, to want to see more of My glory.

Ask, and you shall receive.

I listen to your every request and soak in every voice of praise and love from you. I reveal myself to you when you pursue Me and show myself when you search for Me with all your heart. I fill the empty heart with incredible riches from My storehouse. I have reserved riches just for you that will bring joy and immeasurable pleasures.

Seek, My adored one. Seek, and you shall find.

"Then you will call upon Me and go and pray to Me, and I will listen to you. And you will seek Me and find Me when you search for Me with all your heart." Jeremiah 29:12-13

I am your rock

My beautiful and worthy one, I know you need something to give your life meaning. I am aware the world you see and live in is changing fast. Nothing stays the same in the land of shifting sand. However, I came to this land as a man because of you. I wanted to be near you and save you from eternal destruction.

I loved you so much that I could not let anything stand between us. I made way for you to know Me and live your life through Me so you would know meaning and purpose. Do not expect the world to understand how you can find your purpose and true self in Me. If they do not have Me in their heart, they will not see the value in what you have.

Living life through Me and in Me and because of Me is the only way to live for today and all eternity.

Come to Me My Bride and discover more.

There is always something new in My world. Some discovery, revelation, purpose, or a new passion will bring you incredible joy, filling you with abundant hope for today and always.

I am waiting for you to ask of Me. I wait for you to come and sup with Me, and we can talk about what I would have you do and be. I will give you all you need to fulfill the plans I have for you. You are not alone in these high pursuits for Me and My glory.

Be filled. Rejoice that I have it all under control, holding you steady in the shifting sands of this temporary world.

I am your solid rock.

The best is yet to be. I long to share it all with You. Come and know real life in Me.

"In this, the love of God was made manifest among us, that God sent His only Son into the world, so that we might live through Him." I John 4:9

I deliver you from all battles

My redeemed one, many are the battles and afflictions of the righteous, but I deliver victoriously out of them all.

The weapons the enemy forms against you may look challenging, sometimes piercing your heart. But I keep my hand on your heart, protecting you from his onslaughts. Indeed, his glittering weapons are nothing more than cheap cardboard covered with aluminum foil compared to My unbreakable armor that I put on you.

I know you are weary of the battle. I know you have fought hard and long.

Rest in Me.

Rest even though you must stay alert to his moves. I watch with you and give you weapons in My Word to fight.

The battle is won in Me!

Carry the victory in your speech and heart. Train your mind to listen to My voice. And you shall have peace even though the war wages on.

You are My warrior and have My strategy to win every battle.

You do not fight alone.

You do not rest or hide alone for you hide in Me and find the safety you need.

No weapon formed against you can prosper!

I have demolished all weapons and plans of the enemy. Please stay on the side of victory by listening to My voice. Receive My instruction. Obey quickly with no hesitation. Study My word in times of peace so you will have it in your spirit during testing. Then the pressure of the battle, through the power of the Holy Spirit, will move My truth to the forefront, and you shall obtain the victory you want.

"No weapon formed against you shall prosper."
Isaiah 54:17

I know the feeling of betrayal

My Beloved, I know how it feels when close friends betray you. I know the deep pain when someone you laugh and cry with, eat, talk with, forsakes you. This type of wound goes deep! Since I understand and know firsthand, I can comfort you.

Come to Me with this aching in your heart.

It is okay to cry. I will not hurt you further but lovingly hold you, binding up your wounds. I have the perfect ointment for all body, heart, and soul troubles.

I suffered as you suffer.

I walked the same road as you. My feet felt the familiar sharp stones on the hard ground of this world. My eyes saw My friends run away, leaving Me alone in my time of need in the Garden. My ears heard the awful cries of the people I came to rescue, "Crucify him! Crucify him!"

Still, I loved those who betrayed Me.

I died and rose from the dead not just for the faithful ones but for all humanity. And because of Me and My power in you, you can love those who hurt you too. When they hurt you, I will heal you. When they betray you, I come closer, reminding you of My faithfulness. Do not fear them, My child. You have Me always. And I am a faithful God, a perfect Father, a loving friend who sticks closer than a brother, forever.

"There are friends who pretend to be friends, but there is a friend who sticks closer than a brother." Proverbs 18:24

I encamp around you

My child, you honor Me by inviting Me to be your protector. I come and set up camp around you to keep and guard you in all your ways. Ask Me, and you will see that I am good, an ever-present help in times of trouble.

My dear one, I know that you are often afraid. I am near. You need not fear the unknown, for I am in control of what you cannot see. I have eyes like an eagle. I can see changes in weather and emotions that might come your way.

Come to Me, and I will lift you high above the struggles into a haven of love and security in Me. Stay with Me when the storm rages around you, and I will comfort you.

I do not expect you to be strong apart from Me. When you meet with Me and taste and see that I am good, you will know the strength you long to know. Things of the world only tantalize the taste buds and temporarily fill the stomach. But I go beyond physical needs and fill the empty soul with courage and supernatural strength.

Come to Me. Honor Me. And you shall have all you need for life and godliness.

My love whispers strength to you in all areas. You can then share that love with those who do not know.

You are strong in Me so go and give it away today.

"The angel of the LORD encamps around those who fear Him and rescues them. Taste and see that the LORD is good; How blessed is the man who takes refuge in Him! Fear the LORD, you, His saints; For to those who fear Him there is no want." Psalm 34:7-9

I am your hiding place

My dear child, I know when you need to rest.

I know when you need to feel My arms of love around you. I invite you to crawl into My lap, and I will comfort you. I will hold and gently rock you until you are again at peace. The going can get rough, I know. I am the God who will minister to you when you are in distress, giving you rest and energy to go out there again and win.

There is no condemnation if you faint from weariness. I will help you up. I will stay with you and teach you to walk again without falling. Perhaps not all gently led you when you failed, but I am not like a man.

I am patient, loving, and kind.

My compassions fail not. Do not look at how others may have hurt you in their treatment of you and think I am like them, for I am not.

I forgive.

I love even when I am not loved in return.

I keep your dreams for you when you are unable to dream anymore. My mercies fail not. My love does not run dry. My affection will not go to another when I have set My heart on loving you through thick and thin, in good and hard times.

I am a faithful God.

I never sleep! If you are awake in the night, so am I. Talk to Me! Shut out the distractions and fellowship with Me. I can give you a drink that can sustain you beyond any drink this world serves.

I can give you food that will minister to your most profound need, for I made you and know what you need. It is not too late. I am still reaching out. See Me, My love. See Me and come into the arms of your loving Father. I will wait here for you.

"You are my hiding place; You will protect me from trouble and surround me with songs of deliverance." Psalm 32:7

I know your hearts cry to have a baby

I hear the cry of your heart, My child. I know the longings that you have—longings to be a mother. I understand your disappointment when another season passes, and you still have not had a child.

I have not forgotten you. Nor am I passing you by unnoticed. I am a covenant-keeping God. Ask Me, and I will show you riches you do not know.

I will show you My heart, my love that surpasses all understanding.

I give drink to the thirsty soul and feed the hungry heart. I want you to be a part of My grand plan to give hope to those crying out to Me now. I want to use you to dry their lonely tears. I will advise you and give you all you need. Your joy is magnified when you hear My love in the sound of new voices and responsibilities. I remember you and have not become hard of hearing. All your prayers, dreams, and tears are sealed in My heart. I will answer.

Be at peace. Have faith and wait on Me for the perfect answer in My perfect time. There is a time for everything. Your time is coming.

"Sing, O barren one, who did not bear; break forth into singing and cry aloud, you who have not been in labor! Enlarge the place of your tent and let the curtains of your habitations be stretched out; do not hold back;

lengthen your cords and strengthen your stakes. For you will spread abroad to the right and to the left." Isaiah 54: 1-3

Love with the love I give

My child, I know that it is not always easy to love. It is tough when you are mistreated and misunderstood. I understand how it feels. My life mission was to show the world the love I had for it. I came to save the world. But My actions and words were twisted by many and repeated in a way that made Me look like I only had hatred and condemnation for humanity.

Still, I loved them. And so can you. The love I give you has supernatural qualities and goes beyond feelings.

My love is a verb. I so loved the world that I gave. And this is the kind of love I have put within your heart. I want the world to come to Me and know My love. They know My love by watching you and your love for them.

They will know Me by knowing you. When others hurt you, come to Me, and let Me minister to you. I can give you what you do not have.

When you are mistreated and misunderstood, My love for you is secure. It is nice to have approval and feel love from others, but when you do not, you always have My unchanging love.

Come to Me when it hurts, and let My love be big in you. I died to show you the depth of My love that goes as deep as you need it. I give it to you so you can give it to others. For My glory give. There will always be more love and grace, more peace and hope. You can do all in love, for you are complete in My love, whose well will never run dry.

"Let all that you do be done with love." 1
Corinthians 14:16

My love is eternal

My sweet one who cannot rest though night has fallen, and all is still, I hear the words you cannot say.

I feel the pain you cannot feel.

I see your path before you though all seems dark, for I am your ever-present light. I do not sleep, so there is not a moment when you are alone. Answers may seem hidden from you but are not hidden from Me.

Come to Me and rest in My arms. The way has been challenging. The hours have been long that you have sat up and eaten the bread of sorrows, but I am here to give you peace.

I watch over you and sing songs of hope and safety. Each song that I sing to My children is unique. Not one sounds the same. All who listen for My still, small voice and hear the song I sing call the song Love. Listen, and you will hear that all is well.

You will catch the words from My heart that sings—

Do not fear, My child. I will hold your tomorrow. I gently lead you on in the way you should go. You go nowhere that I have not already been. You walk no path that I have not already trodden. You will see no sadness that I do not already know. You do not walk alone.

Your cries have come to My ears, and I have turned up the sound of My love in response. Can you hear it? Come closer and listen. It is your song—a love song from Me to you telling of a faithful love that will not end. Listen. It is sung just for you, for now, and for all eternity.

"I call out to the LORD, and He answers me from His holy mountain. I lie down and sleep; I wake again because the LORD sustains me."
Psalm 32:4-5

I love you regardless of your emotions

My precious Bride, I adore you. When I see you, I see the one whom My heart loves. I enjoy the bright smile when you are happy, feeling like all things are possible. I am with you on those days when you succeed and things go as planned, but also, I am there on the days when things go awry.

The hard days do not mean that I have left you, for I have promised never to leave you even if you do not call on Me. I still speak words of love and encouragement on those days, but often you do not hear My still small voice that longs to bring comfort. Too often, the enemy of your soul convinces you that I do not care. The truth is there is no way that I could ever stop caring for you. Listen carefully for My voice when all you are hearing are negative words. Speak the truth to yourself about Me, and the enemy voices will fade.

My words bring healing to your soul. They are sweet and pleasant to taste.

My plans for you are plans of peace and prosperity.

I have loved you with everlasting love.

I will never leave you or forsake you.

Do not fear, for greater is He (Me) who in you than he who is in the world.

If I am for you, who can be against you? I am the friend that sticks closer than a brother.

Weeping may endure for a night, but joy comes in the morning.

Speak My words, meditate on the truth, and you shall have the strength to get through the hard days joyfully.

"Pleasant words are a honeycomb, Sweet to the soul and healing to the bones." Proverbs 16:24

Daily I provide

In the rugged valley of decision, My precious Bride, look to Me for direction.

Trust Me with the future you cannot see or know for I see it and know it. And it is good! You need not take on tomorrow's worry, for today is enough for you.

Daily I shall supply all your needs.

Daily will I direct your steps and your thoughts.

Keep your mind set on Me. Keep your feet pointed in the way I instruct you to go.

You will not miss My voice whispering directions to you in the coming days. I know the days are evil, and fear sometimes grips your heart, making it hard for you to move in any direction.

Rest.

Breathe, and let Me speak to you. Allow me to lead you to peaceful waters and green pastures. I am your Good Shepherd and will never leave or forsake you.

I do not slumber but watch you and your loved ones at night.

Worship Me when you feel afraid. Sing to Me when you are uncertain. I will fill you with all you need for the journey. I keep an abundance of riches for you and will give them to you when the time is right.

You shall not wander forever, and your home is with Me always.

Trust in Me, the One who gave you life. Have faith that I will lead you safely home.

I see and know. And I will provide.

"Trust in the Lord, and do good; Dwell in the land, and feed on His faithfulness. Delight yourself also in the Lord, and He shall give you the desires of your heart. Commit your way to the Lord, trust also in Him, and He shall bring it to pass." Psalm 37:5-6

I am the great encourager

My precious loved one, do you need encouragement? Please find it in My word. Then encourage others with words from Me, and you will be encouraged. Give, and you shall receive. I love to see My children speaking words that lift another, words that enlighten and speak truth into a situation. I am glorified when My word goes forth to the downhearted and the weak, and they, in turn, receive new strength and hope to go on. I wish to use you this way in a more excellent way. Do not think that someone else will do it.

I know you have heard My voice many times and spoke to the lonely and lost. You have delivered that word to them, fitly spoken like apples of gold in settings of silver. The way you stepped out gladdened My heart! Be an example to others who do not know how to be a light, who feel like they have nothing to offer. Show them that because they have My spirit, they can speak a word that will bring blessings to the hearer.

Do not be fooled by how the ones in need may appear. Hear the cries. See the emptiness in their soul that may not be heard with physical ears or seen with physical eyes. When you spend time listening to My voice, you can better hear the voice of those who need encouragement.

Encourage one another! Be Me to each other, and you shall, in turn, be encouraged.

"Therefore encourage one another and build one another up, just as you are doing." 1 Thessalonians 5:11

Rest in Me

Oh, My child, time spent resting in Me is not wasted. The world you live in wants you to believe that you must always be doing to be successful. That is not My way. I spent many hours alone with My Father when I walked the earth as a man. We had such a sweet fellowship, and I wish the same for you. How can you give My love away if you have starved yourself? How can you go the second mile with another soul when you have not walked a mile with Me alone? How can you tell a friend that I am enough to meet their needs when you have not come to Me with your needs so that I can fulfill them from My riches? I want you to have enough love, power, hope, and joy; all you will need to live the life I have for you.

I do not expect you to give away what you do not have.

Do you know it is okay to just come to Me with no words? It is okay to fall at My feet and cry. I will not abandon you. I will not condemn you and tell you to get over it. I will come to where you are, touch you, and minister to you. I know what makes you cry. I am aware of the most significant worry in your mind and heart. Come and let us talk about it. Look to Me, and you will see only love coming from My eyes. You will soon begin to feel My strength seeping into you. Soon you will feel strong enough to rise and go. And I will go with you!

Come and rest. Patiently wait with Me and in Me and for Me. I long for you and will wait, My forever love.

"Rest in the Lord and wait patiently for Him."
Psalm 37:7

You will know victory

My mighty Bride, do not fear the battle that is before you, for you do not fight in your own strength. You battle in My power for My glory. It is I who fight for you. And I have already won. The struggle may seem intense; at times, it may look like you are losing ground, but you are not. Ask Me to show you how things look from My perspective, and I will.

Many heavenly forces are working to bring about victory. The forces of darkness have no authority over a child of God. See Me big in you, for that is what I am. Seek to know the power you have in My name and use that power. When you feel weak, I will send helpers to help you stand, just as I sent Aaron and Hur to hold up the arms of Moses. (Exodus 17)

The enemy's words cannot hurt you if you do not let them get into your spirit. Counterattack every negative word of the enemy with the truth from My word.

If you hear "You will lose," say "I am victorious in Jesus."

If you hear, "It is of no use." Say, "God makes all grace abounds towards me so that I will have enough for every excellent work."

Fight with the power of My Word as I did. "It is written." Do not let the enemy get the last word. My word is power. I always do what I have ordained.

Go in Me. Go with My word in you, and you shall know victory.

"Greater is He that is in you than he that is in the world." 1 John 4:4

Healing is for you too

My beautiful Bride, healing is for you too. I know you have come to Me many times asking for healing. Each time My answer was yes!

I have not passed by you.

I have heard your cry. And I have healed you. Sometimes the manifestation of that healing takes a while, but it is not because I am refusing your request.

My plans for you are always for good and not evil, to give you a future and hope. Stay with Me. Stay in My presence, and I will whisper My secrets to you. I will pour out My love to you that goes beyond your physical need. I wish to hear your voice. I long to hear your heart and have you near Me in prayer and worship.

See Me in My word and be encouraged with who I am. I am the same, yesterday, today, and forever. I will go the distance with you. Sometimes I will give a doctor wisdom that will help in the healing. Other times I will speak to you and give direction in the areas of health. The body and the mind are fine-tuned instruments and I, as the master creator of them, know what is best. I wrote the manual for each person's physical body. I understand all. I know all.

Wait on Me. I am the God who heals. Do not stop asking to see, for you shall have what you wish. Time is of no limitation to Me, and I am never late. Trust. Be at peace. I am here.

Then Jesus said to him, "Rise and go; your faith has made you well!" Luke 17:19

You are free

My dear one, no failure has to enslave you forever. I have come to set you free from the past, things that have held you back.

You are not a prisoner any longer. I have opened the door of the past and led you out. You do not have to go back there ever again. I give you strength to walk free.

Often when a person is freed from a situation, old memory tapes continue to play. I have a new song for you to play! It is in My word. Listen to it daily, especially when past pains and failures come knocking on your door. You do not have to answer the door but can stand firm by speaking My word. Man does not live by bread alone but by every word that proceeds from the mouth of the Lord.

"You did not receive a spirit of slavery that returns you to fear, but you have received the Spirit of sonship, by whom you cry, "Abba! Father!" (Romans 8:15)

Speak My word into the past, renewing your mind, and you will then be free to walk into the fullness of the good plan I have for you.

My love for you is immeasurable! I have so much for you! Come to Me with all of you and taste and see that I am good. Whom the Son sets free is free indeed.

"The steps of a good man are ordered by the Lord, And he delights in his way. Though he

falls, he shall not be utterly cast down; For the Lord upholds him with His hand." Psalm 37: 23-24

My compassions fail not

My beautiful Bride do not despair. You shall see what I have shown you in your heart with your eyes. It is coming. Do not weaken in faith, for it will not be too late. You have believed, and your faith shall be rewarded.

How could I forget the cry from the heart of My child? You are so precious and lovely to Me that I have forever engraved your face on the palm of My hand. Others may have forgotten, but I can never forget.

My compassions fail not. I remember that man is but dust.

Wait on Me.

Wait in Me.

Wait for Me, for I shall surely come.

Ask for more of My power, My miracles, My provision. I love it when you ask Me; I love to answer. The storehouse of My blessings is full. Ask, and you shall receive. Do not stop asking. Ask for more of Me, and you shall have all other requests.

Know that My ways are not your ways. But My ways are not beyond your knowing. Like a loving father, I give to those who come the closest to Me and look to know My heart. That is where the most incredible joy lies. As you come to know Me and My heart, your own heart will grow in courage. You shall discover My goodness which will make your heart soar beyond anything you could imagine.

Wait for Me, for I will surely come to you.

"I would have despaired unless I had believed that I would see the goodness of the LORD In the land of the living. Wait for the LORD; Be strong and let your heart take courage; Yes, wait for the LORD." Psalm 27: 13-14

I love you!

My beautiful Bride, you are altogether lovely to Me. When I see you, I see My heart in full display, for I created you, and you are perfect. I know you do not always see yourself this way, but I cannot help but see you. I created you in My image. You are continually before Me, ever visible to Me. I carefully choose each molecule when I knit you together in your mother's womb. No part is randomly thrown together. No part of you is a mistake. I love what I have created! I breathed life into you and watched in amazement as you took that first breath. You are Mine! At no time did I ever regret the works of My hands. At no time did I look away from the loveliness of your face.

I love it when something makes you laugh. I laugh with you. I enjoy it so much when you are happy and singing, dancing before Me in praise and worship. My angels dance with you. They give a lift to your steps and watch over you carefully. Even on days that are not so good, you are still the sweet apple of My eye. So much awaits you!

In My kingdom, you are honored. You sit high with royalty, for you are My Bride. Flowers adorn your head. Jewels of red, blue, and purple lay a pleasant path for your feet. Calm waters of life flow near you; every tree is green and suitable for eating. You are Mine. Come and sit with Me, and you shall see that I am the God who stores up good things for His faithful ones, and that is what you are to Me.

"For You created my inmost being, You knit me together in my mother's womb. I praise You because I am fearfully and wonderfully made; Your works are wonderful; I know that full well." Psalm 139: 13-14

I am your strength

My child, hope in Me when you have no hope left. I will not disappoint. I understand how easy it is to grow weary. Life is hard, but I have overcome this world and all the trouble that goes with it, and so shall you. I do not grow tired or weary. But I understand how you can, for I, too, was a man. So, I am the perfect One for you to come to and find strength. Do not go to the world to find what your soul needs, for that will only leave you emptier. Come to Me first, and I will direct you.

The eagle is mighty and finds strength and power by going higher; it is the same for you. Like the eagle, lock your wings and go higher in Me, allowing Me to take the controls in the storm, and there you shall find supernatural strength.

Have no fear, for in Me, you are stronger than the enemy.

Through Me, you can see what you could not see on your own.

With Me, you can keep running and not faint when others have fallen.

Walk on with Me by your side, and you will not fall.

'Do you not know? Have you not heard? The LORD is the everlasting God, the Creator of the ends of the earth. He will not grow tired or weary, and His understanding no one can fathom. He gives strength to the weary and increases the power of the weak. Even youths

grow tired and weary, and young men stumble and fall; but those who hope in the LORD will renew their strength. They will soar on wings like eagles; they will run and not grow weary; they will walk and not be faint."
Isaiah 40:28-31

You need not fear

My precious Bride, you are not alone when you need shelter. Just as I know when every sparrow of the sky falls, I am aware of all your activities. I never take My eyes off you. You are My lovely one. My love and protection of you are utmost in My heart, and I will not let you down.

You can trust in My unfailing love!

Storms can be hard to endure, but I come nearer to you at those times, pulling you closer to Me. You need not fear. No eternal harm can ever come to a child of God who trusts in Me for salvation.

Abide in Me, and you shall thrive!

I do not expect you to produce fruit on your own. I invite you to come closer to Me, know Me, and grow into Me. I see what you can become when your roots go deep in Me. I am a sure foundation. In Me, you will find all you need for life. Even if you try and survive without Me as your vine, My love for you will not change. I want what is best for you. I am your fortress, and My door is always open. Stay with Me, and you will discover who I am. My love is calling you today. What your heart desires is what I will give you.

Abide in Me, My lovely one.

"He who dwells in the shelter of the Most High
Will abide in the shadow of the Almighty. I

*will say to the LORD, "My refuge and my
fortress, My God, in whom I trust!" Psalm 91:1-2*

Let Me refresh you

My child, life is stressful, and the soul and the body grow weary. I want to lead you to a place of rest and restoration—a safe place of peace and where there is more than enough for your needs. Sometimes it is necessary to get away and get alone with Me so you can hear Me. It may seem dark and confusing in the rush of activity, but all is clear in My presence. It is not wrong to want to have uninterrupted time with Me - it is necessary. I know people and situations in your life need immediate and constant attention. Ask Me how I can help you with that, so you can come away and be with Me.

I long to refresh you and give you rest.

The journey with Me has stops and resting points along the way. Needing to slow down does not mean that your passion for Me has died but that it is necessary to get refueled. I am guiding you. Everyone runs in the race, and I want you to win!

Rest in Me beside the still waters. Lie down in the green pastures with Me. Stay until you are full, feeling the power of My love flowing through you once again. Then you will lack nothing and have all you need to finish strong. My love is drawing you. Come away.

"The Lord is my shepherd, I lack nothing. He makes me lie down in green pastures, he leads me beside quiet waters, he refreshes my soul. He

guides me along the right paths for his name's sake." Psalm 23:1-3

I will protect your heart

My dear one, I gave My life for your heart. I understand how the heart hurts and needs healing. I am the God who heals you. You do not have to hide the hurt from Me. I already know what you feel. I have come to set you free, not further enslave you.

You are free in Me.

You are whole in Me.

I have devised a way for your heart to stay protected during the storms of life. The remedy for all sorrow and struggles of the heart is My word applied liberally and often.

My word will wash you and convict you, direct you and instruct you.

It will warn, prepare, thrill, and sustain you.

It is straight from My heart to your heart. I long for you to know more about it, so it will become such a part of you that it spills out when you talk with your friends, work, or walk in the park enjoying the lovely scenery. Or when you are deep in meditation, alone in your room, or when you are out shopping.

My word will train you, test you, and set you free. You keep your heart by knowing and keeping My Word. All things are possible if you believe, and the more of My Word in you, your faith will grow. Think about it! Think about Me. And you shall be secure, full of hope, and able to encourage those who have fallen. Grow in My word, and you will soar like an eagle as I reveal more of Myself to you. It is all there for you, My child. Keep Me, and you, in turn, will keep your heart. Then you shall know the joy of honest living. You will know abundant life in Me now and for all eternity.

"Keep your heart with all vigilance, for from it flow the springs of life." Proverbs 4:23

You are My joy

My Bride, keeping your eyes on Me will get you where you want to go. I am always looking at you. My eyes fill with love beyond the love of any human on earth. My words whispered in your ear are words of endless encouragement. I would never lead you down a path that would bring destruction to you. I suffered when I carried the sin of the entire world, but I knew I would gain you. I said, "Yes!"

You are the joy set before Me! I can now aid you in the race. I can help you let go of every weight slowing you down. I do not condemn but love you into the person I have called you to be—the person you want to be.

You do not run alone. Many are cheering, praying for you, and encouraging you to keep running. Many have run on the same road as you; they have felt the pebbles in their shoe bringing them pain. They know the agony of sore legs, an aching head, and a tired heart. They made it, and you will make it, also.

Look at Me! I am there with My arms open wide! If you slip and fall, I help you up. If you fall again, I help you up repeatedly and again. It takes what it takes. The day is coming when the race on earth will end, and you will rest forever in My presence. Until then, I run with you, and you shall be victorious.

"Therefore, since we are surrounded by so great a cloud of witnesses, let us also lay aside every weight, and sin which clings so closely,

and let us run with endurance the race that is set before us, looking to Jesus, the founder and perfecter of our faith, who for the joy that was set before Him endured the cross, despising the shame, and is seated at the right hand of the throne of God." Hebrews 12:1-2

Choose life

My Bride, when you praise Me in all circumstances, you show Me that you trust Me even if you do not understand. You are saying that you still love Me and will follow Me even if the way is confusing. Because of sin and man's free will, many things not of Me happen on earth. All men must choose life or death. I am pleased that you have chosen Me and life. I shall bless you forever for that choice. Until then, rejoice in Me! I have things under complete control. You do not have to understand all I allow to worship Me for who I am. I am pleased that you have chosen to trust Me in all circumstances.

When you worship Me when it is hard, I move in and inhabit your praises. I give you what you need to go on and help you let go of those things that are too hard to understand. I am your perfect Father, and I will never leave you. You are not an orphan; you belong in My family. I will come to you and give you peace that passes understanding. Be of good cheer, for I have overcome all in this world, and with Me in you, so shall you!

Dance, My child, dance, I love to see you dance and worship Me. I feel your love. I see your heart and am so pleased that you want to step into the place of deep intimacy with Me.

Dance when you do not understand.

Dance when you do understand.

Dance when you are lonely and when you are not. I am the Lord of the dance and come near you when you draw near Me.

Dance, My lovely Bride. Rejoice in Me, and again I say rejoice!

"Rejoice in the Lord always; again, I will say, rejoice." Philippians 4:4

Come to Me

My dear one, I am your peace in chaos and uncertainty. I am your lifeboat when it feels like you are drowning in anxiety and trouble. When things are spinning out of control, I am your peace. I am the truth when lies surround you. I am life though death is all around you. I am hope where there is despair. I am all and have all you need for life. This world will never give you what you hunger for or need. Since I created you, it makes sense that I would know what you need in every moment of every hour of every day. To obtain what I have and what I am, come to Me.

Come to My well that never runs dry.

Shut out the negative news that is always there and the depressing thoughts and let Me speak peace to your mind. I wait for you to come to Me, and we will walk beside still waters and rest in green pastures. Tell Me what is in your heart. Think of your best friend who had time to listen to you without judgment; who understood what made you laugh and knew what brought tears to your eyes; who loved you and might even give their life for you. Then take that person as an example and magnify it a million times, and you will have a picture of my love for you. I am ever present! I will not leave you. Quiet your thoughts and hear My soothing voice of love ministering to your most profound need. I am in control of all things.

Come to Me, and I will restore your soul.

"Cast all your anxiety on Him because He cares for you." 1 Peter 5:7

Sing My Child

My loved one, My promises never fail. My love does not fade. It is not based on your performance but on the finished work on Calvary that made way for all men to know Me and live eternally with Me.

You shall sing, and no one can stop the sound! It has reached My ears. I am pleased with its melody. The earth rejoices at the music of My children that I have forever redeemed from the curse. You are part of that glorious number.

Sing, My child, sing for joy, and all of Heaven and earth will sing along.

Do you know that you are altogether lovely to Me? You are the apple of My eye, My heart's desire! I have so much planned for you! Raise your voice in worship to Me. Join in with the multitude of other lovers and sing loud and clear. If you listen carefully, you can hear the rumble of the sound of a new song. You have a part in this song. You have a special section that only you can sing. You have come close to Me in worship; now it is your turn to sing. I have not forgotten all you have asked of Me. I know the lovely sound you make when music erupts from your soul. Get ready. It is time to rejoice in the song.

Sing, My love, sing! Go out with joy. Go forth in peace and sing the song I have put within you!

"You will go out in joy and be led forth in peace; the mountains and hills will burst into

song before you, and all the field trees will clap their hands." Isaiah 55:12

I am your peace

My beautiful Bride, I am the God of peace. I speak peace to your heart and mind. Worry cannot change one thing, but I can change all things. Roll all your stress on Me. Do not hurry through your quiet times with Me but savor those sweet moments when I speak My love to you. Like a good friend you enjoy chatting with over coffee, I wish to have you linger long in My presence. My presence is not only available for short periods in the morning, at night before bed, or at church. It is good to seek Me at those times, but I created you to acknowledge Me with you always. I am in My word, and in that still small voice you hear when you are quiet and listen.

My presence goes with you, wherever you go and whatever you do. I am an ever-present God.

I care about all that concerns you. In My presence is where you learn to trust. Trust when things do not make sense to you. Trust when you must wait for the answer. Trust when the way is hard, and you cannot see My hand. You can know My peace in all situations. My peace I leave with you, and it is not as this world gives, but it is perfect peace that passes all understanding. You can know it even if you do not understand it. Come and rest awhile with Me and let Me sing to you. I will sing a beautiful song of love to you. I will take all your anxiety. Breathe deep of Me, My love, and you will find the rest you desire. I love you so much!

"You will keep in perfect peace those whose minds are steadfast, because they trust in You."
Isaiah 26:3

My love is unconditional.

Do not worry, my dear one; I have things under complete control. I know your heart is heavy with everything you want to do for Me. I am incredibly pleased with your request asking Me to use you as a light in the dark. I am answering little by little every day.

I want you to know that My love is not dependent on what you do. Your performance does not change how I feel about you. I love to use My children, but more than that, I want all My children to know beyond any doubt that the place I have set for them at My table is secure. There are days when you may feel that you have failed Me. That is not possible! I do not measure accomplishments in a ministry or calling the way this world measures it. Faithfulness to whatever I have called you to, whether it appears successful or not, is cause for celebration! One person that is changed for the better and feels My love because of you is enough to get Heaven rejoicing!

I shall open new doors to you, but please know that the door to My heart is always open. I love you just as you are, whether on a mission field or at home feeding your pets and sending cards to loved ones. My love just is!

All I have called you to will happen, so do not fear. Hear My still, small voice daily, and I will direct you.

"For everything, there is a season, and a time for every matter under heaven." Ecclesiastes 3:1

You are perfect

My lovely child, you are perfect to Me just the way you are. Do not look to someone else and measure yourself as a success or a failure. I do not do that when I see you. You are lovely and talented and gifted in just the perfect way. Perfect for My plans. It can be hard to hear My voice and direction when you compare yourself to someone else and put yourself down. I wish to plant you in fertile soil, so you will grow into the lovely flower I have made you to be. I have the perfect spot to place you on the windowsill of My glory. Come to Me and let us talk about this. Take your eyes off how I have gifted and am using others, and look to Me. You matter!

You have incredible worth, and I want to show this to you.

No one can bloom like you! No one has the colors and the aroma like your petals and branches have! Come to Me and thrive in Me as your forever vine of love. You shall bear much fruit if you remain in Me. Excellent fruit that you are not even aware of now. I know just the right amount of moisture and sunshine that you need. Your roots go deep in Me, and I will complete what I have begun.

You are altogether lovely to Me, My beautiful Rose of Eternal Love!

"When they measure themselves by themselves and compare themselves with themselves, they are not wise." 2 Corinthians 10:12

My food brings life

I have food to eat that you are not aware of, food for your soul. You have not because you ask not. Come to Me and eat what is good. Come and dine on that which will bring abundant life in Me.

I see you looking around, asking, "What shall I eat? What in this world can satisfy my soul?" I am there with the table set for you. I am in your wilderness when you feel you are all alone and all have forsaken you. I have set a table of choice foods to satisfy your deepest needs. I know just what you like. I know what would be too rich for you and make you ill or what would be too bland for you and make you restless. I have perfectly seasoned it all for you. And it is just what you need for the task I have set before you. My food is life-giving. It is served on silver platters by My angels. I sit at the head of the table next to you, My lovely Bride!

Come to My table and eat what is good! Your table of plenty shall appear in the wilderness when you least expect it. It will not be too late but right on time. Seek Me and eat what is good.

"Come, all you who are thirsty, come to the waters; and you who have no money, come, buy and eat! Come, buy wine and milk without money and without cost." Isaiah 55:1

Come to Me

My dear child, your weakness is not something from which you must run. Its purpose is to cause you to run to Me and exchange your weakness for My strength. You have tried to hide from this weakness or make excuses as to why you have it but has this helped you overcome it? I am the God who helps in your weakness.

Come to Me; I shall create strength out of your very weakness.

I am not ashamed of you and the struggle you have. I know all about it anyway. I am there to love you, heal you, and make you into a mighty warrior—a warrior who will carry the victory in Me to others who are still struggling.

Do not fear. Do not panic.

Lay it all down at My feet and see what I can do. Humble yourself, and I will lift you. And when I lift you up, you are changed. You will have the aroma of My presence on you. Even if you resist Me and My help, I am still there, extremely near you. I know you will not find lasting peace or help in anything or anyone outside of Me.

My love knows no end. My strength is beyond anything that you can imagine. I died for you so you could know Me and the supernatural power available to you. By letting Me be God in this area, you are saying yes, Lord, yes, and this dependence will bring much joy to you and glory to Me.

"That is why, for Christ's sake, I delight in weaknesses, in insults, in hardships, in persecutions, in difficulties. For when I am weak, then I am strong." 2 Corinthians 12:10

Seek My face

I am calling you away to Myself, so you can discover more of what you need to live the life I have called you to live. It is not to condemn you or bring up your mistakes and failures. It is to love and heal you in the areas you need to feel My touch.

My love is calling you away. I want to speak words of life and hope to you. Sometimes the world's noise gets too loud for you to hear My voice. I have not left or abandoned you! You are My precious child. I know you have experienced painful things that made you doubt My love. I know you want answers from Me as to why they happened. Some things are too high for you to understand now. But you can know My presence, peace, and everlasting love. I wish to hold you and fill you with more of Me. All shall be clear in the end. Come to Me and let Me speak to you. Seek My face, and you will find what satisfies you. You do not walk alone. Nor do you cry alone. You cannot wander too far away in a storm of the mind and emotions for Me to reach you.

Seek My face and live.

Seek My face and understand.

Come to Me, My love, and let Me love you. I will wait for you. Come as you are. You will not be disappointed.

"You have said, "Seek My face." My heart says to You, "Your face, Lord, do I seek." Psalm 27:8

I have the final word

My child do not fear man and his opinion of you that changes daily. Trust Me. My opinion of you does not change. I have chosen to love you with an everlasting love. I will complete what I have begun in you. People can run short of patience and are not always loving, but I am always patient and loving. I always have your best in mind.

When you place a person's opinion above Me, you risk making an idol of them. Reverence Me. Yes, I speak through man, but My voice in your spirit is more significant than man's voice. I alone have the final word. If someone tells you that you are hopeless, that you will always fail at life, that I will never open the door of ministry or provision to you, and you embrace that opinion, then that is not of Me.

If a man tells you, you have used all My mercy, he is not standing for Me. For it is impossible for My mercy to run dry. When you come to Me and ask me for help, I will not turn you away. I will answer when you ask Me to change you and fill you with strength and power.

Man is fickle. They praised me one week and the next, yelling, "Crucify him! Crucify him!" Likewise, you will never always have people's approval through no fault of your own. Seek My approval. Look to know and understand Me. Seek to discover My plan for your life and then pursue it. Do not worry if others agree with what I have called you to do. Your path is unique. If you make a mistake or take a wrong turn, I am always there directing you back to the path I have for you—a path of peace and prosperity. I can see what is dark and tangled to you. I will make your path straight. Look to Me for direction and wisdom. Do not become trapped in seeking man's approval. Seek My approval only, and you will know peace.

"The fear of man brings a snare: but whoever puts his trust in the Lord shall be safe."
Proverbs 29:25

www.ingramcontent.com/pod-product-compliance
Lightning Source LLC
Chambersburg PA
CBHW071223090426
42736CB00014B/2955